PORT LLIGAT
SALVADOR DALÍ
HOUSE-MUSEUM

Text by: Antonio Pitxot / Montse Aguer.

Graphic design: Jaume Romagosa.
Translation and Photocomposition: Editorial Escudo de Oro.
Photomechanical Reproduction, Printing and Binding: FISA ESCUDO DE ORO.
Distribution: Comercial Escudo de Oro.

I.S.B.N. 84-378-2004-9.
Legal Deposit: B. 10291-2004.

Carlos Pérez de Rozas.

"A LIFE WITH THE LIGHT OF ETERNITY"

Antonio Pitxot / Montse Aguer

FUNDACIÓ
GALA - SALVADOR DALÍ

INTRODUCTION

Dalí's relationship with Cadaqués began early in his life. His father, a notary public, was born in the town and had a house at Llaner beach. Dalí spent holidays there and treasured wonderful memories of the place, associating it with summer and free time when, far from his studies, he could devote himself to painting. In his early diaries, Dalí often recalled Cadaqués with melancholy from wintry Figueres. For example, on 8 January 1920 he wrote: «I spent a delicious (summer), as always, in the ideal, dreamlike village of *Cadaqués*. There, beside the Latin sea, I feasted on light and colour. I passed the burning summer days painting frenetically, endeavouring to translate the incomparable beauty of the sea and the sun-drenched beach. Later, 23 April 1920, he added: »I think of Cadaqués and feel a great sensation of profound tran-

quillity. Summer evenings…painting… nights warm with moon, with longing, of a silent love… reflections and the blue of the sky, of the sea…the white of foam, happiness! A fishing boat making its way back and the shining of the first star of the evening…» (*Un diari: 1919-1920. Les meves impressions i records íntims*, 1994). Dalí, then, associates summer, art and Cadaqués. In view of the young Dalí's sincere enthusiasm and interest in art, his father leased a studio for him, which was formerly used by the artist Ramon Pichot i Gironès, not far from the family home. This was a large, whitewashed room at the top of a fisherman's cottage, overlooking the bay near Sa Cueta beach. The walls were still hung with sketches and drawings by Pichot i Gironès, a member of a family of intellectuals and artists closely linked to the Dalí family. During the 1920s, Dalí spent most holidays at the family house in Llaner, which became a meeting-point for the young artist's friends and acquaintances. Federico García Lorca visited the Dalí house in 1925 and 1927, and other illustrious visitors included the guitarist Regino Sainz de la Maza, who Dalí also frequented at the Students' Residence in Madrid, and the writer and journalist Carles Costa, who coined the expression «putrefacts.»

1929 was a decisive year in Dalí's life: it was in that year that he met Gala, soon to become his life's companion and muse. Dalí spent the summer in Cadaqués, where he was visited by the art gallery owner Goemans and his companion, Luis Buñuel, René Magritte and his wife, and Paul Eluard and Gala, with their daughter Cécile. When the party returned to Paris in September, Gala stayed on for a few more weeks in Cadaqués, and from that moment on was always by the painter's side. This relationship and an article by Eugeni d'Ors published in *La Gaceta Literaria* on 15 December 1929 describing Dalí's provocative attitude at his first exhibition in Paris, were the reasons behind the rupture of the artist's relations with his father.

The Dalí family on the beach at Llaner in around 1910.

Federico García Lorca and Salvador Dalí at the Dalí family house in Cadaqués.

Port Lligat in 1930, with the fisherman's hut Dalí bought from
Lídia of Cadaqués.

THE ORIGINS OF THE HOUSE

Due to the above-described reasons, in 1930 Dalí was
looking for a home of his own, and finally moved into a
cottage in Port Lligat sold to him by Lídia Noguer, of
whom Dalí wrote in *The Secret Life*: «Lídia was a woman
of the village, the widow of Nando, the good sailor of blue
eyes and the serene look. Her age was about fifty. The
writer Eugeni d'Ors had spent the summer once, when he
was twenty, in the house that Lídia owned at the time.
Lídia's had a mind predisposed to poetry, and had been
struck with wonder at the unintelligible conversation of
the young Catalonian intellectuals.»
Dalí further wrote that when d'Ors published his well-

known book *La Ben Plantada*, steeped in neoplatonism,
«Lídia said immediately: 'That's me.' She learned the
book by heart, and began to write letters to d'Ors in which
symbols presently appeared with alarming abundance.
D'Ors never answered these letters. But he was at this time
writing his daily column in the *Veu de Catalunya*, and
Lídia became came to believe that this column of d'Ors's
was the detailed, though figurative, answer to her letters.»
Dalí went on to explain the reason for his fascination with
this personage: «Lídia possessed the most magnificent
paranoiac brain aside my own that I have ever known.»
The house was, in truth, little more than a shack, its ceiling in poor condition, and was used by Lídia's sons to
store their fishing tackle. In an interview he gave in 1954,

Dalí told how he came to discover Port Lligat: «I lived in Cadaqués, and went up and down the coast with my brushes and my canvases until one day I came across a shack. From that time on, I never had to carry my painting things to and fro all the time. That shack became my present home.»

As for the economic side of the question, Dalí's patron, the Viscount of Noailles, accepted the young artist's proposal that he should advance him 20,000 francs in exchange for a painting which finally turned out to be «The Old Age of William Tell.» Dalí used the proceeds to purchase his new home in Port Lligat.

In order to narrate the origins of the house in Port Lligat, we must once more turn to *The Secret Life*, in which Dalí describes all the details of the evolution of what was to be his residence for over 50 years, situated in the place he most loved in the whole world. Firstly, Dalí describes the site and the landscape: «This shack stood in a small port, Port Lligat, which was a fifteen minutes' distance from Cadaques, beyond the cemetery. Port Lligat is one of the most arid, mineral and planetary spots on the earth. The mornings are of a a savage and bitter, ferociously analytical and structural gayety; the evenings often become morbidly melancholy, and the olive trees, bright and animated in the morning, are metamorphosed into motionless gray, like lead. The morning breeze writes smiles of joyous little waves on its waters; in the evening very often, because of the offshore islands which

Lídia Noguer, *La Ben Plantada*, and Dalí in Port Lligat.

Gala with Lídia Noguer's sons.

Dalí and Gala at Port Lligat in the 1930s.

Dalí and Gala in the Port Lligat house in 1931.

make Port Lligat a kind of lake, the water becomes so calm it mirrors the dramas of the early twilight sky.»
Dalí then goes on to describe the difficulties of moving from Paris to his new home in Port Lligat: «We took the train at the *Gare d'Orsay*, loaded as bees. Ever since I can remember I have always wanted to travel with my documents -that is to say, with some ten suitcases stuffed with books, photographs of morphology, insects, architecture, texts, endless notes. This time, moreover, we brought a few pieces of furniture from our Paris apartment, and a whole collection of butter-flies and leaf-insects mounted under crystal, with which we planned to decorate the house; also gasoline lamps and heaters, for in Port Lligat there was no electricity. The instruments for my painting made a whole pile of baggage by themselves, among which a large revolving easel stood out.»

The artist continues with his description of the difficulties they experienced in reaching Port Lligat and moving into the new house: «From Cadaques to Port Lligat, the road leads between abrupt rocks, where no car can get through. So it was necessary to carry everything on a don-key's back. It took us two days to get settled, and during these two days we lived in a continual fever. The walls were still all damp, and we tried to dry them a little at a time by turning the heat of our gasoline lamps on them.»
Finally, of the house itself Dalí writes: «We hired a car-penter and together Gala and I worked out all the details, from the number of steps there were to be in the stairway to the dimensions of the smallest window. None of the palaces of Ludwig II of Bavaria aroused one half the anx-iety in his heart that this little shack kindled in ours.

«The shack was to be composed of one room about four metres square, which was to serve as dining-room, bedroom, studio and entrance hall. One went up a few steps, and on a little hallway opened three doors leading to a shower, a toilet and a kitchen hardly big enough to move around in. I wanted it to be very small -the smaller, the more intrauterine. We had brought the nickel and glass furniture from our Paris apartment, and we covered the walls with several coats of enamel. Not being in a position to carry out any of my delirious decorative ideas, I wanted only the exact proportions required by the two of us and the two of us alone. The only extravagant ornament which I planned to use was a very, very small milk tooth of mine which had never been replaced, and which I had just lost... I wanted to pierce a hole in it and hang it by a thread from the mathematical centre of the ceiling.»

Dalí also makes numerous references to his plans for life with Gala: «We talked about being alone, to see what was going to happen between us. Down there we were going to

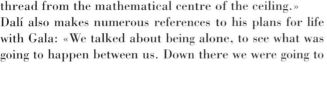

Interior with functionalist furniture, 1931.

Dalí and Gala on the terrace in Port Lligat, with the bay in the background, 1931.

build walls in the sun to protect us against the sun, wells to catch springs of water, stone benches to sit on. We were going to build the first steps of the critical-paranoiac method; we were going to continue that tragic and beautiful labour of living together, of living for the reality of just the two of us!»

Once installed in Port Lligat, and far from Parisian society and its activities, they began to an ascetic, isolated life. As Dalí writes: «It was there that I learned to impoverish myself, to limit and file down my thought that it might become effective as an ax, where blood had the taste of blood and honey the taste of honey. A life that was hard, without metaphor or wine, a life with the light of eternity. The lucubrations of Paris, the lights of the city, and of the jewels of the Rue de la Paix, could not resist this other light -total, centuries-old, poor, serene and fealess as the concise brow of Minerva.»

Dalí ends his description as follows: «Gala and I spent whole months without any other personal contacts than Lídia, her two sons, our maid, Ramon de Hermosa, and the handful of fishermen who kept their equipment in their shacks in Port Lligat. In the evening everyone left for Cadaques, even the maid, and Port Lligat remained absolutely deserted, inhabited solely by the two of us.»

ARCHITECTURAL GROWTH

Dalí himself provides the key to understanding the intricate structure and the surprising labyrinthine arrangement of the Port Lligat house: «Our house in Port Lligat has grown just like a true biological structure, by cellular additions. Each new event in our life corresponds to a new cell, a room. The nucleus is the fruit of the delirious paranoia of Lídia, who gave us the first cell as a gift.» Our first references to the house are found in some interesting letters from Lídia to Dalí in 1930. These narrate the origins: on 8 June she writes to him in Paris to inform

Dalí, Gala, Paul Eluard and Nusch on the terrace in Port Lligat, 1931.

him that the house is ready and painted, and that the painter has given her the key to the «Barraca» (shack) so that she can install the basics in it. On 14 June, she reports that she has bought the kitchen furniture and the table; on 17 June, she mentions that they will take some cutlery and crockery to the house, and that she has found the girl who will help them. Finally, in a letter dated 24 June, she reminds him that they are going that day to his father's house in El Llaner to get his furniture. On 20 August 1930, Dalí officially purchased Lídia's shack, measuring around 22 square metres, and on 22 September that same year, he acquired a second shack of a similar size. First of all, Dalí put the hut bought from Lídia in order, building a terrace roof on which he installed a huge parasol, and opening up an oblong window, framing the landscape outside. He rehabilitated the second hut in 1932, this first cell of the house serving at once as entrance, dining-room, living room, studio and bedroom. A short flight of steps led to a tiny kitchen and a small bathroom. Built over the rock with dry stone walls, these huts had roofs made from ceramic tiles. It was in this space that Dalí and Gala received the visit of René Char, Paul Eluard and his second wife, Nusch; Valentine Hugo, and René Crevel, who was to spend long periods here in later years.

In 1932, the house comprised the two huts and a small annex, now the office. In the olive garden he built two rows of small cylindrical columns to form what would be the site of many and varied events and the setting for photographs for over 30 years, as well as reinforcing some of the benches there with tiled backs.

In 1935, Dalí and Gala decided to extend the house, contacting the builder Emili Puignau who, from this time on, carried out all the construction work they commissioned. Puignau it was who built the two units corresponding to the studio, now the Yellow Room, and the bedroom, now the Bird Room, finally completed the following summer. The work entailed finding solutions to numerous technical problems, two in particular concerning the arrangement of the house: it is a very tall building, constructed on various different levels. Moreover, Dalí and Gala were to remain in it whilst the work was carried out,

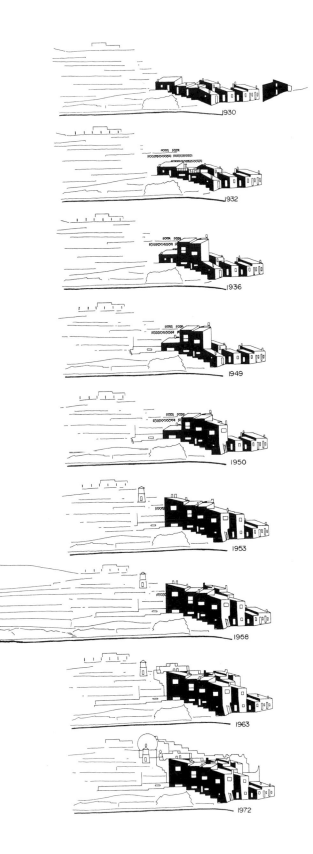

The evolution of the Port Lligat house in nine stages (study by Oriol Clos for the catalogue of the exhibition *Dalí. Architecture*, Barcelona, 1996).

Gala and Dalí on the *Via Làctia*, or «Milky Way», wearing the costume of the giants at the Beistegui dance (Oriol Maspons).

making it impossible to remove the roofs. Needless to say, Dalí was interested not only in practical questions, but also in the aesthetics of the alterations, as the same techniques were to be applied to the entire construction of the house. For example, Dalí declared that the roofs should form a series of steps as if leading down to the sea. An additional problem was that the walls could not take any overloading, as there was nothing anchoring the stones of which they were built. For this reason, Puignau constructed reinforced concrete supports over the dry stone walls.

On the outbreak of the Spanish Civil War, Dalí and Gala moved to live in the United States and did not return to Port Lligat until the end of 1948. Over this long period of absence, the painter's family looked after the house. In 1944 Dalí's father, the notary public, wrote to his son to tell him that the painter Josep Maria Prim and his wife,

a close friend of Anna Maria, would be staying at the house until they came back from the United States, adding that they would repair all damage and take care of the garden. We know that Prim and his wife were living in the house in September 1944.

In 1948, Dalí and Gala bought another shack, also some 22 square metres in size. This was converted into the present library and living room in 1949. They also purchased a piece of land which was later to form part of the olive garden.

Puignau carried out this second extension, following the artist's instructions (they worked without the services of an architect), transmitted in the form of letters, sketches, designs and drawings. By the spring of 1949, the house was ready to receive the couple. Gala looked after the decoration of the house and bought numerous pieces of furniture from antique dealers in Olot and La Bisbal. From 1949 onwards, the house grew in accordance with the needs of Dalí. A live-in maid was also hired, so that the house had to be extended yet again and a separate entrance built. Three more huts were incorporated, and over the 1949-50 period a new studio, the present, definitive studio, was built and finally completed in the spring of 1950. In 1951, with the kitchen practically complete, a bedroom began to be built over the library. Other servant's quarters were added in 1952. In 1954, the dovecote was built, whilst the following year Dalí bought the so-called «clock hut», which was kept just as it was until the modernisation which converted it into the cloakroom of the house-museum.

As regards the *Via Làctia*, we find a first reference to this «Milky Way» in *Diary of a Genius*, written in 1956, and, two years later, in 1958 -the year the work was carried out- Dalí spoke of it once more. The Milky Way was a white limestone path running parallel to the sea, the point where it begins marked by a pomegranate tree. The Oval Room was completed in 1961. This room, as its name indicates, is practically hemispherical in shape, its design based on an idea of Dalí's, dating to the year 1957, for a banqueting room in Acapulco. The patio and the surrounding wall, designed to make this space inaccessible, were built in 1962, the summer dining-room in 1963 and the swimming pool, planned in 1969, was completed over the summer of 1971, though Dalí continued to work on it, altering certain of its elements. This peculiar site enjoyed its period of period of maximum splendour, becoming the centre of Dalí and Gala's social life, from 1972 to 1974.

On 30 June 1982, the day Gala died, Dalí shifted his residence to Púbol Castle, abandoning Port Lligat forever.

The spectre of sex-appeal, 1932. Dalí Theatre-Museum, Figueres.

Dalí in the dovecote, whitewashed and designed, like the whole house, by the artist. (Melitó Casals, Meli).

THE HOUSE IN THE LIFE OF THE PAINTER

A visit to this House-Museum is indispensable for all those who wish to attain a profound vision of the iconography of Dalí. This is true both for the house itself and for the landscape which surrounds it, a landscape to which the artist was intimately linked from his infancy and which closely resembles that of his dreams. The fantastic geology of Cap de Creus was a particularly important source of inspiration to him. The Port Lligat house is the work of Dalí, a Dalí who sought solitude and peace in order to paint. It was the only stable residence he had, the place where he resided habitually, for six or seven months a year. His life was spent between Port Lligat, Paris -where he stayed at the Hotel Meurice- and New York -where he took apartments in the Hotel Saint Regis. Port Lligat was, then, where he lived, painted and planned, and where he produced many of his most important works and where he had his studio. The structure, the spaces, the

peculiar organisation, the overall concept of the house, were designed by Dalí, but it was Gala who chose the furniture and ornaments, who imbued the dwelling with an oriental spirit. In the exterior, the most striking elements are an immaculate whiteness and the red of the roof tiles, forming the steps of a stairway leading down to the sea. The house was gradually integrated into the landscape, with the giant plaster eggs installed on the roof, the heads of Castor and Pollux, the fork-crutches of the dovecote. Once inside, we find ourselves in a labyrinthine structure displaying true sagacity in the use of the most simple materials: whitewashed walls, slate, esparto matting on steps and floors, and an enormous accumulation of objects giving the entire site a magical, uniquely personal air, defined by Catalan writer Josep Pla in his own inimitable style: «The decoration of the house is surprising, extraordinary. Perhaps the most exact adjective would be: never-before-seen. I do not believe that there is anything like it, in this country or in any other. The decoration of houses is always the same,

according to the social condition of those who live in them: the bourgeoisie, the petite bourgeoisie, etc… It is the common, constant place. They don't exactly rack their brains over it. Dalí's house is completely unexpected. A precise, exact description should be made of it. It contains nothing more than memories, obsessions. The fixed ideas of its owners. There is nothing traditional, nor inherited, nor repeated, nor copied here. All is indecipherable personal mythology. There are many things whose meaning is only known to the owners. There are art works (by the painter), Russian things (Gala's), stuffed animals, staircases of geological walls going up and down, books (strange for such people), common things, sophisticated things, etc.» (*Obres de Museu*, 1981).

It was here, then, that Dalí found inspiration and worked, but he also received visitors from all over the world: Walt Disney, the Duke and Duchess of Windsor, King Humbert of Savoy, his friend and patron Arturo López or Queen Elizabeth of Belgium, to name but a few.

THE HOUSE

EXTERIOR

To find oneself at the entrance to Dalí's house in Port Lligat is to stand on the threshold, to enter, his work. Facing the sea, with that special light, the changing hues of the sky, and the classical, idyllic landscape of Port Lligat, with dragon-shaped Sa Farnera isle guarding the entrance to the bay. According to the artist himself, the light here resembles more that of Holland than that of the Mediterranean: for Dalí, Port Lligat is, from the point of view of light, a Mediterranean Delft.

Moreover, Dalí liked to place important historical events in this beloved spot. He had heard, for instance, that Charles V had been forced to spend the night here with his fleet due to the fierce storm caused by the *tramuntana*. What is known for certain is that during his first sea voyage Philip II, Charles' son, spent the night of 3 November 1548 in Cadaqués, sheltering from a terrible storm.

Port Lligat, with its string of interlinking islets forming a tiny bay, is a place imbued with a strange sensation of nostalgia which in the evening becomes impregnated with an air of sadness evoking in us Böcklin and his *The Island of the Dead*, that work which so fascinated and obsessed the Surrealists. Dalí, captivated by this atmosphere, planted hundred-year-old cypresses right beside the house. These trees grew alongside the walls, giving a Romantic, Böcklinian air to the entire scene. Meanwhile, ever-present in the background is the headland known here as Cap de Creus and which is, in the words of the artist, «exactly the epic spot where the mountains of the Pyrenees come down into the sea, in a grandiose geological delirium. There, no more olive trees or vines. Only the elementary and planetary violence of the most diverse and the most paradoxically assembled rocks.» It is interesting to recall that, for the artist, «the long meditative contempla-

Midday (1954). The Salvador Dalí Museum Collection. Saint Petersburg, Florida.

tion of these rocks has contributed powerfully to the flowering of the 'morphological aesthetics of the soft and the hard', which is that of the Mediterranean Gothic of Gaudí -to such an extent that one is tempted to believe that Gaudí must, at a decisive moment of his youth, have seen these rocks which were so greatly to influence me.»

Turning now to the immediate surroundings of the house itself, our attention is drawn particularly by the effect caused by the conjunction of the boat and the cypress tree.

The boat is emblematic, romantic, whilst the tree inside it is, a well-known symbol here, for the ship's mast has the same name as a tree in Catalan. Dalí took these allegories and gave them a literal sense full of personal connotations. The boat-cypress forms a single ensemble with a fountain, the meeting-point of hippies during the 1970s. This fountain, surrounded by legend, appears in various works by Dalí, including the *Portrait of Gala with two lamb chops balanced on her shoulder*, painted in 1933.

The "Clock Hut", now the cloakroom of the House-Museum.
The painted doors, an example of abstract art.

In the cloakroom is the dry stone hut with the sundial -
an icon present throughout his work, and particularly
significant in *Noon* (1954)- acquired by Dalí and conserved just as it was installed by the fishermen of
Cadaqués.

Still contemplating the exterior of the house, we now turn
to the painted doors, whose origins are interesting: Dalí
always used to ask the local fishermen, when they finished painting their boats, to finish off their paint and
dry their brushes by painting the doors. This custom was
employed as a way of saving materials, and Dalí liked it
because, as he said, this technique had led to the creation
of the best abstract pictures in the history of painting.

Another element here, found on the floor and leading us
towards the entrance to the Port Lligat house, is a fish,
designed by Dalí and made from slate, placed vertically,
as in the old paths around Cadaqués, with a prominent
eye and a marked backbone.

THE HALL OF THE BEAR

Entering the house through a tiny, narrow door, the first room we come to is known as the Hall of the Bear.

This tiny chamber, corresponding to the original hut bought from Lídia of Cadaqués, is presided over by a stuffed polar bear which formed part of the decoration in his Rue de l'Université apartment in Paris during the 1930s. This bear, which welcomes visitors, is the house totem, giving a foretaste of the atmosphere we will find here. Dalí adorned the bear with necklaces, medals and a variety of walking sticks, some of them extraordinary pieces, one of them, African in origin, made from ebony. Amongst these walking sticks is an item of outstanding interest: a 15th-century German harquebus used by the artist in 1957 for some of the lithographs he produced to illustrate *Don Quijote*. The bear serves as a lamp, holding a torch made from a fisherman's *gambina* (a large net made from reeds), letter-holder and umbrella stand.

Behind the polar bear is an owl and some framed butterfly wings, its ocelli echoing the gaze of the owl, symbol of wisdom. The 18th-century cupboard, Catalan with Provençal influences, is crowned by *semprevives* – everlasting flowers, a herbaceous plant which grows abundantly in the Cadaqués area. Gala loved this plant, which is also present in the interior of Púbol Castle.

To the right is an Isabellina-style armchair, covered in the same material as the sofa, a Modernist table and an elegant little table made from bull's horns, its foot formed by three interlaced horns.

On the wall is a crossbow and two reproductions. The first of these is Giorgione's *Tempest*, present in the entrance to his house because, according to Dalí, it is the most mysterious picture in the history of painting: it features two people separated by a river, and no one can know what strange conversation is going on between the two. Below this is a portrait entitled *Don Joseph de Marguerit et de Biure -Marquis d'Aguilar Sr. de Caftel Gral. des Armes*, with a large mustache. Dalí used to claim that he collected mustachios, particularly famous ones. This interest has its origins in Adolphe Menjou and his mustache, about which he used to joke with Luis Buñuel during their time at the Students' Residence in Madrid.

Under the window is the famous sofa shaped like a pair of lips designed by Dalí himself. Another version of this sofa also forms part of the Mae West installation in the swimming-pool area at the Theatre-Museum in Figueres, whilst yet another is also found at Púbol Castle.

On the floor is an imitation tigerskin rug.

Dalí and Gala in the dining-room. In the foreground, the
candelabras designed by the artist.

THE DINING-ROOM

Leading off from the left of the entrance are two more
rooms, the dining-room and the library. These form a
space without doors, and are communicated by two narrow corridors. Here we can appreciate fully the differ-
ences in level between the original fishermen's huts. The
esparto mats, made in Figueres, are the ones used on the
roads for carriages in bygone times.

The dining-room and entrance form the first cell of the
house. The former is an austere space where meals were
normally served. Dalí also used to call it the «petit refectori».
It was in this room that Dalí began painting his works

dating to the 1930s. As there was no electricity, he painted by the light coming in through the skylight and, when
it got dark and this was insufficient, that of a *petromax*
lamp, a system used by fishing boats for working at night.
The room is presided over by the fireplace. Built by exca-
vating into the rock, this was one of the first fireplaces
designed by Dalí. Side-by-side, a row of wicker chairs of
different sizes on which are an equal number of straw
bowler hats, forming an ornamental effect similar to that
of a Russian doll. Gala's influence is also apparent in the
presence of the everlasting flowers and radiator screens,
made from an old wall cupboard.

Particularly interesting are the table and the 17th-centu-

ry bench. The two candelabras, designed by Dalí, are in wrought iron. On the wall is a photograph of Velázquez's portrait of Philip IV.

Our attention is now drawn by an enormous poster for a bullfight featuring Paco Camino, Curro Girón and Fermín Murillo, which the city of his birth dedicated to the painter in 1961 as part of a series of events organised in Figueres on the occasion of his designation as favourite son. In the centre of this poster is a drawing by Dalí representing a bull being lifted by helicopter, a project the artist wished to see carried out, but which was made impossible by the strong *tramuntana* wind which rocked the city on the day. Dalí was convinced that all dining-rooms should contain the representation of a bull being carried off into the heavens by helicopter as, in his view, food should be elevated vertically towards God. Opposite is a rustic-style lamp-holder created by the artist himself and which he used in the 1930s to hold the *petromax* lamp from which he obtained artificial light for painting. Amongst the numerous objects displayed here, particularly interesting are the decorative elements garnered during his walks by the sea and around Cap de Creus. Sea animals are often present in his works: seagulls, seashells, lobster, starfish... Other ornamental elements he especially liked were corncobs; the «weather friar», in the fireplace; the polychrome carving representing the head of Saint John, and the enormous wickerwork basket.

Finally, we turn to the shelf placed under the skylight which gives the room its light. This shelf is full of a vast number of bottles whose aesthetic beauty caught his attention. Both the shelves and the fireplace are finished in chalk and whitewashed.

THE LIBRARY

Going up five steps, we come to the library but, before reaching it, we find, on the right, a small window giving a different, new view of the fireplace in the dining-room. The library, also used as a living room, corresponds to the third hut acquired by Dalí and known as Ca l'Arsènio. Its most interesting elements include the wooden bookcase installed high above the fireplace, and which runs the entire length of the wall. Against the opposite wall is a wooden bench dating to the 18th century. The books, dealing with a varied range of subjects such as art, architecture, literature, philosophy, physics, medicine, mathematics, the natural sciences... are now housed in the Centre for Dalí Studies at the Gala-Salvador Dalí Foundation in Figueres, used for reference by scholars studying the life and work of the Master. At the back was the Espasa encyclopaedia. Every night, Dalí would have a volume brought to him, reading to discover new concepts to analyse and study in depth. The walls are also hung with reproductions of two of his works: *Cadaqués*, 1923, and *Port Alguer*, 1924, Cubist interpretations of a landscape close to his heart.

Dalí was concerned to conserve the three swans which used to nest in the bay of Port Lligat and which even wore, at times, a kind of little cap which would be lit with a candle and which stayed alight until the birds put their heads into the water. Dalí, of course, was always fascinated by mythology, and one of the motifs recurrent in

Dalí posing in the library (Gyenes).

Dalí, reading, in the library, 1951.
(Ricard Sans i Condeminas).

Port Alguer, 1924. Dalí Theatre-Museum, Figueres.

Dalí and Gala in the library, seen from the terrace
(Ricard Sans i Condeminas).

his work is that of Leda and the swan, an element of his iconography which is extensively represented in the Theatre-Museum in Figueres.

The two armchairs where Dalí and Gala would often sit to talk, read or contemplate the landscape, along with such other ornamental elements as the eagle standing on an old rectory cupboard, the polychrome wooden warrior's arm holding a small collection of flags, including those of the countries with which Dalí was most linked, or a baroque carving of the repentant Mary Magdalene and a reproduction of a deposition from the cross («Particolare della Deposizione») by Rafael, create a personal, unique atmosphere, the whole presided over by the broad window giving a magnificent panoramic view of Port Lligat bay, and the presence of Gala's beloved everlasting flowers. The carving of Mary Magdalene is particularly unusual, with the skull and a special *bomb* -which Dalí called the «apocalyptic pomegranate»- used to engrave a series of copper plates used to illustrate the *Apocalypse of Saint John*, published in 1960.

Making our way towards the terrace, we find a baroque gilt easel, used by Dalí in his Paris apartment during the 1930s, with photographs of the swans nesting in the bay, of the artist in the summer, and a collage in which Dalí appears with the horse now housed in Púbol Castle. Beside these is a lamp with gilt stand, the work of Dalí himself. On the wall is a photograph of Gala by Horst, published in Vogue magazine on 1 June 1943, along with an article stressing the influence of Gala on the work of Dalí.

Dalí on the terrace (Melitó Casals, Meli).

THE TERRACE

Next, we come to the terrace, its stone walls white-washed, filling it with light, particularly on nights when the moon shines. A mysterious female head is incorporated into the white stone. Looking up, we see the dove-cote, also whitewashed, designed by Dalí. The house was whitewashed every year. Inside, a peculiarly Daliesque formula was employed: Lime was also used, but the water it was mixed with contained ground agaves, giving an irregular bluish tone and making the whitewash last longer. It is interesting also to note that Dalí had the dry stone walls built by experts from Cadaqués in accordance with their own traditional rituals of perfection, after which he had them whitewash their entire work.

On the left is a window affording a panoramic view of the entire bay and also providing shelter from the *tramuntana*.

Though not open to the public, we can see from here, along the «Via Làctia», or Milky Way, a path made from whitewashed concrete paving stones and which runs alongside the sea, a tiny cove known as the *platja d'En Sisó*. It was on this half-hidden beach that Dalí and Gala used to bathe. At the end of the path, lined by pomegranate trees and aromatic plants such as lavender and rosemary, planted by Gala, are her hand and footprints. Turning back, on the left, just before we come to the door to the library, a small opening goes into the rock, with glasses and mirrors which were formerly used to create an optical effect.

THE OFFICE

We now retrace our steps, returning to the «Hall of the Bear». From here, we go upstairs where the first space we find is the office, the kitchen of the first hut. This has a kitchen cupboard containing photographs of various leading members of the Surrealists, as well as of other people of particular importance in Dalí's life: André Breton, Paul Eluard, Dalí and Gala, Freud, Benjamin Peret, Yves Tanguy, René Crevel, Trotski, Max Ernst.

Beside it stands the white sideboard where the cutlery and crockery were kept. This room also once contained a small refrigerator and a television, which Dalí did not enjoy watching.

Also interesting here is the chessboard floor, with black and white tiles. This is a clear allusion to Vermeer of Delft, and similar floor designs are found elsewhere in the house and at Púbol.

TOWARDS THE STUDIO

Continuing our visit, we come firstly to a reproduction of Dalí's *Atomic Leda* (1949) and then to an area of the house in which the rooms are communicated by stairs, narrow openings or tiny corridors. This makes it difficult to see how each is situated with relation to the other, but also gives a feeling of space. This space is original, isolated and intimate, the exclusive domain of the painter: an appendix to the studio.

The first chamber we come to is presided over by a Japanese parasol and crowned by enlarged reproductions of sea urchin skeletons -Dalí used to say that the sea urchin, its form based on the dodecahedron, is a perfect animal, the image of heaven- and two enormous reproductions of Millet's *Angelus*, a key work in the development of Dalí's critical-paranoiac method. Also notable, on the left, is a photograph of the Dalí family: his moth-

Atomic Leda, 1949. Dalí Theatre-Museum, Figueres.

er, Felipa Domènech; his sister, Anna Maria, and Dalí as a boy. The room is also full of a variety of objects: a butterfly-lamp, a Modernist bust-mirror, masks and, more in the background, a model for a large sculpture which was never finally made: a stuffed swan, a bull-souvenir and a skull on a functionalist style chrome tube table; and, in the raised section of the room, various tapestries and a row of candles imitating a fireplace but which are, in reality, electric lights.

We now come to a small space with books and the model of an old opera house, with two accesses: that on the right leads to the studio, whilst the second leads to the so-called «Models Room». Immediately on entering the latter, on the right, at the top of some stairs, is a room used to store Dalí's painting materials and equipment.

Dalí with a series of moustachios. Dalí claimed he collected
moustaches, particularly famous ones.

THE MODELS ROOM

The first thing which catches our attention as we enter
this room is, on the right, a table containing a variety of
optic instruments: a magnifying glass, microscope, a slide
projector, a stereoscope and a mirror. All this reminds us
of Dalí's passion for optics and the mysteries of vision.
Dalí, for example, had invented some kaleidoscopic
glasses he could wear during boring journeys.

Over the table is a mirror offering a new perspective of
the room, and which reveal portraits of three famous
personages with mustaches: Philip IV, Stalin and Kaiser
William of German. We can also see reflected in this mirror a photograph taken at Dalí and Gala's wedding in the

Sanctuary of Els Àngels, near Púbol in 1958. At the rear
of the room is a soft with cushions, an ornament constantly found all over the house, and a kind of canopy
which imbues the room with an oriental air.

The moiré paper decoration reinforces the idea of the
optical illusion, with a wavy watery pattern which
changes with the light. The ceiling is ornamented with
gold and red stripes -the colours of the Catalan flag.
Here, Dalí alludes to the fact that Picasso used to sleep
with the Catalan flag - the *quatre barres* - at the head of
his bed.

These rooms abound in completely heterogeneous
objects, many of them personal souvenirs, so numerous
as to defy description.

Dalí in his studio with the oil painting *Christ of Saint John of the Cross*, 1951 (Ricard Sans i Condeminas).

Dalí in his studio with the oil painting *Christ of Saint John of the Cross*, 1951 (Ricard Sans i Condeminas).

THE STUDIO

Returning to the space which serves as the office and turning right, we come to the nerve centre of this area and the most important space in the house, the studio.

This is the third part of the house, organised as the artist's studio. It began to be remodelled in 1949 when, on their return from the United States, Gala and Dalí decided to reside in Port Lligat, and work was completed in the spring of the following year.

An article was published in the magazine *House & Garden* in June 1950 describing the project for the studio in Port Lligat: «Salvador Dalí's new studio, an airy prismatic structure of glass and steel, will shortly be built at Cadaques, Spain. According to the artist, the inspiration for the design was twofold, consisting of Leonardo da Vinci's drawing of the human proportions and a twenty-sided geometric volume called the icosahedron, of which every surface is an equilateral triangle. Mr. Dalí considers this triangle the most beautiful of its species, and the one which 'produces the most complete feeling of calm.' Certain of the triangles forming the sides of the studio will open up at their outside apexes and be supported by Daliesque crutches, like those that appear in so many of his paintings.

«The metal structure, which will be predominantly gold in color, will be lined with olive wood and hung with antique Spanish tapestries». This project was never carried out. Nevertheless, both this description and the ideas Dalí expounded in his treatise *Fifty Secrets of Magic Craftsmanship*, on how a painter's studio should be, make clear his special -and quite understandable- interest in this space, the most important in the house: the place of inspiration, of refuge, of concentration and of work.

This is a light-bathed room with two windows, one giving onto the sea, with views of Port Lligat bay and Sa Farnera, locations which often appear in Dalí's work, the other facing north. Remember that in *Fifty Secrets of Magic Craftsmanship*, Dalí echoes Leonardo da Vinci in advising painters to ensure that their studios

Dalí and Gala in the studio (Ricard Sans i Condeminas).

are situated where they will receive the best possible light.

As regards the landscape and the environment where a painter's studio should be situated, Dalí writes: «you will fall in love willingly, you will fall madly in love for the rest of your life, with the fragment of landscape which you have knowingly decided, through your intelligence, is, amongst all those you love, that which most merits all kinds of sacrifices.»

Upon entering, what our attention is attracted by the verticality of the door, a door designed by Dalí, as is proven by various sketches which have been conserved, in the form of a truncated isosceles triangle. On the left is a series of completely heterogeneous objects but which are, nevertheless, all related to the Daliesque world: a model of the structure of the hydrogen atom crowned by a zoetrope; a plaster reproduction of a neoclassical sculpture, a fencing mask, a Davy Crockett hat and an American football at its feet. In the niche of the fireplace is the porexpan packing-protector of a radio, which Dalí used as a model in his design of the little temple of the swimming pool, and several pairs of anaglyphic glasses. On the wall is a Flemish mirror reminding us of Jan van Eyck's painting of the *Arnolfini Marriage Group*; and a reproduction of Velázquez's *Las Meninas*, with the grid pattern Dalí used both for work and study.

Dalí in the studio with one of the panels of his work *Palau del Vent*, now in the room of the same name in his Theatre-Museum in Figueres (Melitó Casals, Meli).

Dalí in the studio, kneeling in front of his oil *The Battle
of Tetuan*, 1962, which he painted in homage to Fortuny
(Melitó Casals, Meli).

Under the window is the Provençal bench where Dalí
spent hours and hours contemplating the evolutionary
process of his paintings. It was in this studio that he
painted such important works as *The Christ of Saint
John of the Cross* (1951); the *Last Supper* (1955); the
Madonna of Port Lligat (1955); *The Battle of Tetuan*
(1962); *The Apotheosis of the Dollar* (1965); *Tuna
Fishing* (c.1966-67); or *Dalí from behind painting Gala
from behind, eternalised by six virtual corneas provisionally reflected by six real mirrors* (c.1972-73). For
large pieces, as Emili Puignau explains in his book

Vivències amb Salvador Dalí (1995), the painter decided
to have installed in his studio «a metallic frame which,
with a mechanism driven by a switch, would go up and
down as required. The painting was attached to the
frame by clamps and screws allowing Dalí always to have
the canvas at the most suitable height for painting com-
fortably. Previously, he had always worked seated on a
chair. Moreover, the system for packing enormous pictures was done away with, as it was dreadfully compli-
cated, awkward and laborious. Instead, the system was
adopted of gradually taking the nails out of the canvas,

removing it from the frame and then rolling it up in a light plywood cylinder of the same size as the painting, that is, of large enough diameter to ensure that the canvas of the finished painting could not become deteriorated or creased»; this allowed Dalí to paint meticulously, fragment by fragment, without needing to take into account the entire work. On view in this frame now is one of Dalí's last works in progress, a classical figure in tones of gray. Beside it is a reproduction of his stereoscopic work *Gala's Foot* (1974).

On the more conventional easel is a sketch on wood of an angel. Near this are the armchair and chairs where Dalí sat to paint, with his palette and armrest whose handling, according to Dalí himself, was more decisive than the brush itself.

Numerous paintpots, bottles of varnish, of resin, sol-

vents, blotting paper, palettes, paintbrushes and other items in the painter's equipment, along with books and papers on which Dalí which make his sketches and notes, all go to form this artisanal universe, the artist's domain. Dalí spent most of his time at Port Lligat in his studio. He was a tidy person, and used to follow a regular routine. He started work in his studio at sunrise in order to take full advantage of the hours of daylight. Then, after a bath, lunch and a nap -special and very short, and which he called «slumber with a key»- he returned to the studio once more, working until evening. Gala often used to read to him as he painted. From time to time, Dalí and Gala would go with Arturo Caminada, their faithful butler and chauffeur, by boat to Cap de Creus, or they would take long walks around the landscape which so fascinated him.

THE YELLOW ROOM

The space we enter now is reached through an old door. It consists of three sections and is built on three different planes: these are the bedroom, a small room (the Yellow Room) and an intermediate space paved in gray and white (the Bird Room).

The Yellow Room is thus known because its armchairs and seats are upholstered in yellow material. It is a spacious room with views of the sea. At first, Dalí used it as a studio, but he soon began to need more space and so,

when he acquired another hut, this space was converted into a sitting room.

On entering, we are greeted by a draped figure in white relief, integrated into the left-hand wall.

The table in the centre was designed by Dalí; on it is a precious object in the shape of a snail, transformed into a lamp-clock by Tiffany's. The artist associated the snail shape with the skull of Sigmund Freud.

The room contains an interesting mirror, with a black period frame, which had to be installed at such an angle as to allow Dalí, from his bed, to see the light of the ris-

ing sun. This is the mirror featured in the stereoscopic work *Dalí from behind painting Gala from behind, eternalised by six virtual corneas provisionally reflected by six real mirrors*. The mirror intensifies the beauty of the landscape, giving it an almost magical permanence. Careful consideration and study went into the placing of each of the many mirrors present in the house. In this case, the mirror is accompanied by the structure of a grain of wheat, conjuring up the ideas of germination and the birth of day. Opposite are two reproductions: the *Self Portrait*, painted when the artist was seventeen, the original of which is found in the Theatre-Museum in Figueres, and a drawing dating to 1952, a study for *Galatea*.

Going on now towards the Bird Room, we see, on the right, a Gaudian Modernist table and the chair. On our left is the armchair forming part of the same suite. The desk in the corner, made from olive wood, also serves as a radiator screen. On it are a number of fans and a faded photograph of Gala, an adolescent Gala with the penetrating, mysterious gaze so finely described by Paul Eluard.

Here, too, we find the presence of everlasting flowers: throughout the house, all the curtains are crowned by branches of this plant. This was a custom maintained by Gala, a personal touch imbuing the house with a peculiar atmosphere and aroma.

THE BIRD ROOM

Next, climbing up seven stairs, we come to the Bird Room, a space which communicates the Yellow Room with the bedroom.

The Bird Room is thus known because there was always a cage with canaries here. Beside it is a windscreen with three birds painted by Dalí with a light, skillful line. No doubt he painted them when there were still birds in the cage.

To the left are books and glass objects, along with stones from Sa Confitera beach. One of these glass recipients used to contain sweets and flints, and we know that Dalí used to entertain his guests by throwing flintstones on the floor, allowing them to smell the aroma of burnt powder, as well as offering them sweets, which he himself loved and which reminded him of his childhood. When he was

a small boy, he used to go to the beaches of Cadaqués with his mother and Lídia, where they would gather stones, placing them to remark on their peculiarities and exact precedence.

Heading now to the bedroom we find, on the right, an amphora, the gift of the fishermen of Cadaqués. There is also an 18th-century Dutch commode, its lines curved and delicate. Next, at the foot of the stairs, is a fishing net lined with yellow silk to serve as a screen for a wrought-iron lamp, with various paperweights, unusual minerals and a money box or piggy-bank.

Also interesting is the fireplace, which here serves to communicate with other rooms, with floral ornaments arranged in strange and unusual glass recipients. Opposite is a bench with a tapestry reproducing the figure of Pope John XXIII.

Dalí in the Bird Room, before one of the fire-places he himself designed.

THE BEDROOM

Finally, we go up seven stairs to reach the bedroom. In the centre are two polychrome iron beds with bronze adornments. The beds are covered by bedspreads of a red and blue material repeated in the padded canopy. The entire scene is presided over by an Imperial Eagle, a large ring in its beak. The right-hand bed was Gala's, that on the left Dalí's. The curtains, matching the bedspreads, are blue with red borders. On the bedside table are books, whilst on a shelf on the right is an old photo-

graph of Port Lligat in which we can see the old fisherman's huts. In the left-hand corner is a floral lamp of Modernist inspiration.

The immense, sumptuous fireplace, designed by Dalí, is of the most remarkable originality. It is built from tiles which form a huge circle around a white fireplace. The design of the lower opening of the chimney is based on Dalí's theory that the curve corresponds to that of a drop of water before it breaks due to hydraulic tension: «It is the principle of the drop of water which holds together due to a physical law of surface tension, but

which is converted into a cosmic event.» This idea was repeated in Dalí's design for the chimney in the dining-room at Púbol. Around the fireplace are false plaster divans, balanced by small masonry basements and arranged by Gala with the silk of many cushions, two lamps, Dalí's collection of walking sticks and objects made by the artist from silver paper. Dalí often employed this technique to model objects. To the right, our attention is captured by the trivet with the beautiful leather samovar, with its Russian air. Here we also find wicker chairs, as in the Theatre-Museum and at Púbol. In his last years, when his health did not make it advis-

able for him to go up and down stairs, Dalí had a door built in the fireplace which communicated directly with the patio.

Facing the beds is a Castilian-style desk with two candles and a seasnail from which emerges a snakeskin. On the wall is an engraving of *Saint George and the dragon*. On the right is a Catalan-Aragonese cupboard with repro-ductions of a *Madonna* by Rafael; a portrait of the young Gala and Leonardo's *Ginevra de'Benci*. Dalí saw a similarity between the foreheads of these three person-ages, and said that the universe is little in comparison to the breadth of a forehead painted by Rafael. This series of works is completed by a reproduction of *The Saviour and Antoni Gaudí dispute the Virgin's Crown* (1960), and a *Religious Scene*, which also dates back to the 1960s. The books kept in this cupboard were those which Gala used to read to Dalí in his studio as he worked.

The armchair facing the cupboard was a gift from his friend Arturo López in August 1953: «an easy chair that is a copy of a Louis XIV sledge, the back made out of tortoise-shell surmounted by a gold crescent. All this because of the oriental air that imbues the living thousand and one nights with the Galanian biology of our house and its Catalan flowers, our two beds, the Olot furniture, and an extremely rare samovar» (*Diary of a*

Genius, 1964). In order to return his kindness and show his gratitude, Dalí gave López an oil: a painted red rose. Before we leave the bedroom, let us remember that this is the only bedroom in the house: there is no guest room. This is a dwelling designed for two people determined to maintain their privacy.

Turning back we find, on the left, Dalí's bathroom. Austere, it contains a dressing table covered by a blue cloth.

Going down the stairs again, we return to the Bird Room, which gives access on the left to three more rooms:

GALA'S DRESSING ROOM

This room is austerity personified, with a dressing table full of perfumes, little boxes, paints, jars, small items for personal use and a mirror. The dressing table is covered by a white cloth, a decorative element Gala also used frequently at Púbol Castle.

THE ROOM OF THE CUPBOARDS, OR OF THE PHOTOGRAPHS

This is an intermediate room, made up of glass-cupboards with glass doors where Gala used to spend hours

placing photographs and magazine covers of particular importance to her. There are photos of Dalí and Gala with different personalities from the world of art, culture, politics and science, including Harpo Marx; Ingrid Bergman and Gregory Peck during the making of the film «Spellbound»; Paul Eluard, the Duke and Duchess of Windsor, King Humbert of Savoy, Josep Maria Sert, Màrius Cabré, Picasso, Lawrence Olivier, Marcel Duchamp, Luis Miguel Dominguín... There is also a photograph of Dalí with his father, on a panel giving entrance to the Oval Room. Also displayed here are a great many magazine covers, such as the famous cover of a 1936 issue of Time. This was greatly prized by Dalí as the first time he had appeared on the cover of a North American magazine, with all this represented for his establishment and fame.

Oriol Maspons.

THE OVAL ROOM

This was the last large room to be built. It is situated over the office kitchen and the old servant's quarters. The Oval Room is an intimate, almost inaccessible space, as to reach it one has to go through the dressing room and the Cupboard Room. It is one of the few rooms which has a door which once closed, isolates and even hides it behind the panel with the photographs. This was Gala's refuge, where she spent many hours, where she received her most highly-valued visits and where she devoted herself to one of her favourite activities, reading.

The Oval Room, with its large diameter, has the shape of almost three-quarters of a sphere, of a sea urchin shell. Dalí had already conceived the idea of forming an oval-shaped space in 1957, when he was commissioned to

design a night club in Acapulco, though the project was never finally carried out.

The only furniture is an upholstered bench running around the entire room, the work of the designer Muntañola.

Gala decorated the space with a huge variety of totally heterogeneous objects, both on the sofa and in the niches: enamelled miniatures from Russia, stones from Cap de Creus, soft dolls...

In the centre is the fireplace, also designed by Dalí with a niche with ogee arches on either side. In the first niche, on the right, is a photograph of the young Gala with her brothers and sister. In the second is a glass bust of Nero will internal lighting, and a photograph of the King and Queen of Spain with Gala and Dalí. On the left are two Russian icons, which Gala venerated with some devotion, ornamental eggs of different sizes, the symbol of the perfect shape in allusion to Piero della Francesca, and floral ornamentation. One of the peculiar aspects of this room is the striking reverberating effect in the exact centre of the dome. The slightest noise goes quickly round the circle and can be heard throughout the room. The curtains project a reddish light, that on the right also protecting various Daum paste objects in designed by Dalí, that on the left a reproduction of Antonio Canova's *Love and Psyche*.

We now retrace our steps once more to the Cupboard Room where we find, on the right, the staircase which will lead us to the patio and the swimming pool.

Project for a night club in Acapulco, 1957. Published in *Architectural Forum* in November 1957.

Dalí in the patio at Port Lligat, centre of the social life of Dalí and Gala.

THE PATIO

The conjunction between the sea and the house is made above all thanks to the patio. Gala and Dalí spent much of their time here and the patio was, along with the swimming pool, the centre of their social life. This space, sheltered from the wind, conserves the heat of the day until long after sunset. We reach this patio through a labyrinth cut into the rock and whitewashed to form a vertical tunnel with cages for yellow-necked crickets from Olot, a yearly gift from Dalí's painter friend Jordi Curós. Dalí said he was interested in crickets because their son is in their genetic code long before they are born.

Without leaving this corridor we find, on the left, the tiny summer dining-room, with an original horse-shoe-shaped slate table, presided over by ram's horns and a candle. On one side of this austere little room is a rhinoceros head adorned with floral ornamentation and feathers. The window at the rear is, moreover, framed by the ubiquitous everlasting flowers. On the other side are stone shelves with a variety of decorative elements, such as two painted cages for crickets, a miniature wicker chair with cushion, a series of heads, one made from glass, a Daliesque Venus de Milo and a white plaster sculpture reminiscent of that placed under the dome in the Theatre-Museum. Beside it is a piece of furniture covered by a white cloth. It was in the summer dining-room that visitors were received when the weather permitted, where aperitifs were served, and where dinners took place. Amanda Lear and Ambarina Kalachnikoff, two people from vastly different worlds, but both closely linked to Dalí, were two frequent guests.

From here, following the labyrinth, we come to the olive garden with the dovecote, designed by Dalí himself, and decorated with fork-crutches; to a circular installation which was the scene for various performances organised by Dalí, with a skylight of transparent glass and mechanisms for blowing up balloons in the ceiling, and with perforated pottery pieces fixed to the outer wall so as to produce an echoing sound when the *tramuntana* blew, at times with indescribable violence; and the famous *Christ of the Rubbish*, - a large, ephemeral sculpture made from rubbish salvaged from a flood at Port Lligat. Dalí used to say that one should always take advantage of an accident.

Retracing our steps, we find two enormous white flower pots in the form of cups, and three curved seats formerly used to grind grain, ornamental elements perfectly integrated into the patio.

Left, above, is an opening, on a level with the top of the balcony with its Majorcan-style railing. Here is a lavatory with interior illumination, like those which crown the patio of the Theatre-Museum in Figueres. There is also a torso of Phidias' Illisus. This space is protected by mysterious, labyrinthine corridors forming a kind of wall.

We come next to the area containing **the swimming pool.** The first thing we find on entering this section of the house is, on the right, a spring-fountain-container consisting of a fountain of lions -a copy of the Fountain of the Lions in the Alhambra- an elephant and, crowning the entire assemblage, a Diana the Huntress. At the base of the marbled container is decoration in the form of floral elements and fruit. Below, another reference to Diana

the Huntress, dolphins and two children of dreamy aspect, supported at the foot of the container. At the rear is a Christmas crib. Dalí created this montage through an accumulation of ideas, objects and images. A regular feature of Dalí's creative method is to proceed always by accumulation, never by selection.

Continuing towards the little temple of the swimming pool we find, on the right, a Michelin man at the foot of a mysterious personage-alchemist with the philosopher's stone. Next we come to a fountain, also a copy of the one in the Patio of the Lions in the Alhambra, surrounded by bottles in the form of bullfighters and typical *Manolas*.

This area of the house is where one can most appreciate the influence of the North American pop art movement. Here we find another reproduction of the well-known lip-sofa, against a background of Pirelli tyres, Michelin men and two coats of arms, each with six flowers, a Daliesque reference to the Florentine House of Medici.

The swimming pool, though modest in proportions due to lack of available space, is peculiar and luxuriant, like something out of an oriental tale. The principal ornament here is the building, or temple, which stands at one end. Its design is based on the packaging of a radio Gala and Dalí received as a gift and which is now, as we have mentioned, exhibited in the studio. Around the pool were built benches for those watching the bathers, and a table which emerged from the ground, as if by magic, at the touch of a button.

The swimming pool, as Puignau says: «was to resemble the one in the gardens of the Alhambra in Granada, with fountains at either side and even a small reproduction of the Fountain of the Lions (these were his instructions, without drawings or sketches or anything of the kind). Moreover, the swimming pool was to take the shape of an elongated rectangle, with a width of just one-and-a-half metres. In front of the table, a semicircle was to be built of slighter larger diameter than the width of the swimming pool (as if it were a little cap), with steps to make it easy to enter the water to swim at the other end, as it was not straight at the end. I could make two semicircular forms (according to my taste or criteria) so that the swimming pool should terminate harmoniously.»

As for the shape of the pool, though this is phallic, according to Puignau, «Dalí's real intention was that it should be elongated and run vertically to the table and chairs to give a perfect view of the bathers. This made the whole visually very pleasing. Moreover, when they were working, the little spouts at the sides, seen from the seats, made a kind of tunnel of watery arcs. The visual effect, especially at night, was most impressive, because the light, Dalí used to say, gave the area a phantasmagorical aspect.»

It was decided to decorate this part of the house, the body of the building, in the spring of 1968 when Dalí and Gala returned to Cadaqués. As planned for during con-

struction, the old lighting system from the Cap de Creus lighthouse, a beacon made up of various prisms, was installed in the central niche. Beside this, on the right, is an elephant's cranium, a wooden donkey and a lion, this version made of polyester. On the left, an imitation white owl, a lamp, created by the artist, with a form based on the structure of DNA, and a rocking chair, also designed by Dalí. Other interesting features include two chairs covered by white cloths with bows at the sides, something done to please Gala and also found in Púbol. Outside the temple, on the left, at the top, is a camel, a gift from a well-known cigarette company. The serpents are a present from Brigitte Bardot's sister. The decoration is completed by ceramic swan-fountains and oriental cushions. With the lighthouse beacon on, the illuminated lion fountain, the swimming pool spouts and the different ornaments, this space was turned into something out of a garden in the Thousand and One Nights.

This was the scene of many parties. All were welcome, and a vast variety of people and personalities met here, as well as a group of hippies who were in regular attendance. At the end of the evening, Dalí offered everyone champagne, though he himself merely wet his finger as a toast. The olive garden, with the wall reaching the border of the patio - with olives, aromatic plants such as lavender and rosemary, carnations and geraniums- is crowned by the heads of Castor and Pollux, a pool at their feet to collect water, from where it cascades into the swimming pool.

The vegetation here is determined by the local climate and the arid nature of the soil. For this reason, there are few flowers in the garden, even though Dalí loved highly perfumed flowers, preferably white ones, such as nards, jasmine or lilies.

THE BARBECUE

Making our way now towards the exit, we descend some steps to the barbecue, which is presided over by a white-washed plaster sculpture representing the fish-woman. This creature, unlike the siren or the mermaid, has the head, not the tail, of a fish. We are also surprised here by the presence of a telephone booth, one of the first in Spain, from where Dalí liked his guests to phone.

Leaving now, we are bidden farewell on the right by a metallic money box or piggy-bank given to Dalí by the association «L'Amich del poble català» and an enigmatic personage known to Dalí as the «Extra-Terrestrial».

This visit has revealed to us the real, true Dalí. This house is the only home he ever had, and left its mark on his life and artistic career. The house evolved and was transformed with the passing of time and in accordance with the biological and spiritual rhythms of its inhabitants. It grew and expanded like a cellular structure, following the Daliesque principles of accumulation and integration. It is important to bear in mind that the house was constantly extended over a period of more than 40 years. It grew and changed and was transformed with its owners. It is steeped in their vitality and genius. It was here that Dalí found his inspiration and where he carried out his work.

Let us conclude by quoting Pla once more. An article by Josep Pla, written in 1952, stated that: «Dalí, in his house in Port Lligat, is the most Daliesque thing one may imagine. The house resembles him more each day.»

On the death of the artist in 1989, the Port Lligat House-Museum was inherited by the Spanish State, whom Salvador Dalí had named his universal heir. The house remained closed whilst the Directorate-General for Heritage of the Ministry of Economy and Finance carried out restoration work on it to prepare it for opening to the public. This restoration work was planned and directed by the architect Oriol Clos. On 17 September 1997, the house was opened once more under the management of the Gala-Salvador Dalí Foundation.

The Port Lligat House-Museum forms part, along with the Dalí Theatre-Museum in Figueres and the Gala-Dalí House-Museum in Púbol Castle, of the museum complex managed by the Gala-Salvador Dalí Foundation.

View of the Port Lligat house, 1955 (Brassaï).